Growth Stocks

The Basic Investor's Library

Alternative Investments

Bonds, Preferred Stocks, and the Money Market

Careers in the Investment World

Growth Stocks

Investing and Trading

Investment Banking

Investments and the Law

Mutual Funds

Reading the Financial Pages

Stock Options

The Principles of Technical Analysis

Understanding A Company

Wall Street—How It Works

What Is a Share of Stock?

Chelsea House Publishers

Growth Stocks

JEFFREY B. LITTLE

Paul A. Samuelson
Senior Editorial Consultant

CHELSEA HOUSE PUBLISHERS New York Philadelphia

Editor-in-Chief Nancy Toff
Executive Editor Remmel T. Nunn
Managing Editor Karyn Gullen Browne
Copy Chief Juliann Barbato
Picture Editor Adrian G. Allen
Art Director Giannella Garrett
Manufacturing Manager Gerald Levine

Staff for GROWTH STOCKS
Senior Editor Marjorie P. K. Weiser
Associate Editor Andrea E. Reynolds
Assistant Editor Karen Schimmel
Copyeditor Ellen Scordato
Editorial Assistant Tara P. Deal
Associate Picture Editor Juliette Dickstein
Picture Researcher Alan Gottlieb
Senior Designer Laurie Jewell
Designer Ghila Krajzman
Production Coordinator Joseph Romano

Contributing Editor Nancy Welles
Consulting Editor Shawn Patrick Burke

3 5 7 9 8 6 4 2

Library of Congress Cataloging in Publication Data

Little, Jeffrey B.
Growth stocks / Jeffrey B. Little; Paul A. Samuelson, senior editorial consultant.
p. cm. — (The Basic investor's library)
Bibliography: p.
Includes index.
Summary: Examines growth stocks as shares of companies whose sales and profits are increasing faster than their particular industry or the economy in general.
ISBN 1-55546-624-9
0-7910-0313-2 (pbk.)
1. Stocks—Juvenile literature. [1. Stocks.] I. Samuelson, Paul Anthony, 1915- II. Title. III. Series. 87-24482
HG4661.L57 1988 CIP
332.63'22—dc19 AC

CONTENTS

Learning the Tools of Investing

PAUL A. SAMUELSON

When asked why the great financial house of Morgan had been so successful, J. Pierpont Morgan replied, "Do you suppose that's because we take money seriously?"

Managing our personal finances is a serious business, and something we all must learn to do. We begin life dependent on someone else's income and capital. But after we become independent, it is a remorseless fact of nature that we must not only support ourselves for the present but must also start saving money for retirement. The best theory of saving that economists have is built upon this model of *life-cycle saving*: You must provide in the long years of prime working life for what modern medicine has lengthened to, potentially, decades of retirement. This life-cycle model won a 1985 Nobel Prize for my MIT colleague Franco Modigliani, and it points up the need to learn the rudiments of personal finance.

Learning to acquire wealth, however, is only part of the story. We must also learn to avoid losing what we have acquired. There is an old saying that "life insurance is *sold*, not bought." The same goes for stocks and bonds. In each case, the broker is guaranteed a profit, whether or not the customer benefits from the transaction. Knowledge is the customer's only true ally in the world of finance. Some gullible victims have lost their lifetime savings to unscrupulous sales promoters. One chap buys the Brooklyn Bridge. Another believes a stranger who asserts that gold will quickly double in price, with no risk of a drop in value. Such "con" (confidence) rackets get written up in the newspapers and on the police blotters every day.

I am concerned, however, about something less dramatic than con artists; something that is not at all illegal, but that costs ordinary citizens a thousand times more than outright embezzlement or fraud. Consider two families, neighbors who could be found in any town. They started alike. Each worked equally hard, and had about the same income. But the Smiths have to make do with half of what the Joneses have in retirement income, for one simple reason: The Joneses followed prudent practice as savers and investors, while the Smiths tried to make a killing and constantly bought and sold stocks at high commissions.

The point is, it does matter to learn how financial markets work, and how you can participate in them to your best advantage. It is important to know the difference between *common* and *preferred* stocks, between *convertible* and *zero-coupon* bonds. It is not difficult to find out what *mutual funds* are, and to understand the difference between the successful Fund A, which charges no commission, or "load," and the equally successful Fund B, which does charge the buyer such a fee.

All investing involves risk. When I was a young assistant professor, I said primly to my great Harvard teacher, Joseph Schumpeter: "We should speculate only with money we can afford to lose." He gently corrected me: "Paul, there is no such money. Besides, a speculator is merely an investor who has lost." Did Schumpeter exaggerate? Of course he did, but in the good cause of establishing the basic point of financial management: Good past performance is no guarantee of the future.

That is why *diversification* is the golden rule. "Don't put all your eggs in one basket. And watch all those baskets!" However, diversification does not mean throwing random darts at the financial pages of the newspaper to choose the best stocks in which to invest. The most diversified strategy of all would be to invest in a portfolio containing all the stocks in the comprehensive Standard & Poor's 500 Stock Index. But rather than throw random darts at the financial pages to pick out a few stocks, why not throw a large bath towel at the newspaper instead? Buy a bit of everything in proportion to its value in the larger world: Buy more General Motors than Ford, because GM is the bigger company; buy General Electric as well as GM because the auto industry is just one of many industries. That is called being an *index investor*. Index investing makes sense because 70 out of 100 investors who try to do better than the Standard & Poor's 500, the sober record shows, do worse over a 30-year period.

Do not take my word for this. The second lesson in finance is to be skeptical of what writers and other experts say, and that includes being skeptical of professors of economics. So I wish readers *Bon voyage!* on their cruise to command the fundamentals of investing. On your mainship flag, replace the motto "Nothing ventured, nothing gained" with the Latin words *Caveat emptor*—Let the buyer beware.

The Fee well in Shamburg, Pennsylvania, 1868, one of the first U.S. oil wells.

Growth Stocks

Bernard Baruch, an American financier who made a fortune in the stock market in the early 20th century, was often asked what was the key to profitable investing in stocks. He always advised, "Buy low, sell high." This advice has been repeated many times since. It is obvious that a person who buys stock priced at $10 per share and sells each share for $100 will make a very nice profit. But as everyone who has "played the market" knows, there is a catch in Baruch's advice: If the stock does not go up in price, it cannot be sold for a higher price. One of Baruch's contemporaries, a popular humorist named Will Rogers, made this point when he joked: "If the stock don't go up, don't buy it!"

Investing in stocks can bring financial gain; the trick is to choose the right stocks in which to invest. It is hard to predict which stocks will rise in price and which will decline. Investing in growth stocks, the common stock issued by rapidly growing companies, can bring great financial gain. The key to identifying growth stocks lies in analyzing individual companies. This book will explain how companies grow and show how to identify and when to buy growth stocks, using events of the past as a guide.

An employee at an electricity generating station of Consolidated Edison of New York operates a crane. The shares of utilities are income, not growth, stocks.

WHAT IS A GROWTH STOCK?

Although a precise definition of a growth stock does not exist, it is generally described as a share in a company whose sales and earnings are increasing at a rate faster than that of the company's particular industry or the national economy. Many computer-company stocks are growth stocks. In contrast to a growth stock is an income stock, shares in a major company that has a record of strong earnings but is no longer expanding greatly. Shares in utilities, such as telephone and electric companies, are some examples of income stocks.

Although growth stocks can be found in various companies and in many industries, they are generally considered to be shares in an expanding company that is in an expanding industry. Often the company is a leader in its industry. Companies from which growth stocks can be purchased are called *growth companies*, and the expanding industries are called *growth industries*.

There are two types of growth-stock companies. One is the mature, stable, large company in an expanding industry that has had significant profits in past years and has seen an appreciation in the price of its stock. The annual dividends to stockholders from these companies tend to be large. Some stocks of companies of this type are also called *blue chips* because of the companies' high dividend payments and financial strength.

The other type of growth-stock company is the emerging, aggressive, small company that is engaged in a new and developing industry. This type of company shows rapid growth in sales earnings for several years in a row. Its stock has great potential because of the future prospects of the

A railroad construction crew in Washington state, 1885. Railroading was a growth industry in its early years until the mid-20th century when other means of transportation overtook it.

company. It is also volatile; prices rise faster than those of large companies, but they can fall just as quickly when investors no longer show interest in the stock. This type of company either pays small dividends or none at all.

Investing in larger growth companies is normally safer than investing in smaller companies. The sheer size of the company's operations gives some stability to its sales and earnings; its stock price reflects that stability. As a result, if the mature company falls on hard times, its stock price will probably not fall quite as rapidly as the price of a smaller company's stock. On the other hand, its stock price will probably not rise quite as rapidly, either.

Because companies grow and industries change, what is a recognized growth stock in one decade may not be so in another. For example, in the United States in the late 19th century, the shares of railroad, steel, electric, and telephone companies were growth stocks. At that time, their new products and services were in great demand. As transportation by railroad became more popular and economical, service expanded throughout the country, and demand for steel products that were used in the rails and cars was at high levels. Similarly, as more and more people wanted electricity and telephone service in their homes, the companies selling these services experienced explosive growth. Nineteenth-century investors contributed to this growth by buying shares in such companies and made fortunes when they later sold them at much higher prices.

However, once nearly everyone had telephone service and a home wired with electricity, growth in these industries could not continue as rapidly as it once had. Moreover, as automobiles, trucks, and airplanes began to compete as methods of transportation, the growth of railroads slowed, too. Stock in all these industries declined in status and value. Not surprisingly, the growth stocks of today are completely different from those of 100 years ago.

Why Invest in Growth Stocks?

A person with money to invest can choose among a wide variety of offerings. The offerings can be divided into short-term investments and long-term investments. Both offer the possibility of *capital appreciation*, or the increase in the current value of an investment over its original cost.

A *short-term investment* is one that is made for quick capital gains. An investor expects to increase the original amount of the investment in a short time. One such short-term investment is Treasury bills, or T-bills, which are U.S. government bonds. Some T-bills can be redeemed after three months. An investor can also make relatively small but quick profits in the stock market by frequently buying, then selling shares as soon as prices rise.

Long-term investments are made with the understanding that capital gains will not be realized until a period of time has passed—as few as 5 years or as many as 50. Such investments can be made by purchasing bonds from corporations, which can mature after 30 years and provide steady interest payments each year. Another possibility is to invest money in a money-market or regular savings account where it will accumulate interest. Real estate, gold, and art can all be good long-term investments if the value of the property goes up. Individuals can also invest in their own personal business venture, such as a restaurant or catering service.

Growth stocks are another type of long-term investment. They are an attractive investment because, despite the volatility of their per-share prices, they offer the chance for breathtaking capital appreciation over time. For example, an investment of $13,000 in 100 shares of Du Pont in 1922 would have grown to $1.5 million by 1961, not including the $250,000 received in dividends. Eastman Kodak, Minnesota Mining & Manufacturing (3M), and Procter & Gamble were growth companies in 1950. By 1975, a $1,000 investment in each of these companies would have mushroomed to a total of $46,659, excluding dividends.

The possibilities for investing money are vast, but there are pros and cons for putting it in any particular area. The financial situation of the individual investor will determine what kinds of investments are appropriate at a given time.

Mo Siegel, founder of Celestial Seasonings. In 1970 Siegel put his energy and money into an herb tea business that grew by 1985 to be the largest manufacturer of this product in the United States.

HOW DO COMPANIES GROW?

Although companies may wish to grow, rapid growth actually represents a major challenge. It requires planning and organization, and it is costly. Even more important, a company can grow only when there is a demand for its product or service.

There are different ways in which a company can grow. It may involve the number of buildings it uses or staff members it hires, the quantity of products it sells, or the dollar value of its sales. Often growth in one area means growth in another. When customer demand for a company's product goes up, management must find the resources to increase production enough to satisfy the demand. At the same time, the company must maintain its internal controls as well as the quality of its product. Orders for a product may be so numerous that the company may need to expand production facilities or build a new plant in order to fill them. Additional people must be hired to do the work. The company may want to open new sales offices and sign on new dealers to sell the product. It may also want to increase the amount of money spent on advertising so that more people will know about the product. A company may even want to try to develop related products and sell them, too. All of this growth costs money.

Raising Money for Growth

There are several possible ways for a company to raise money for its growth. Depending on its industry, age, and numerous other factors, the company's management will decide which of the following methods to use.

Borrowing Companies can borrow from individuals or banks. In addition to borrowing from friends and family, many new companies turn to *venture capitalists* to borrow money. Venture capitalists are people with large amounts of money that they use specifically to fund new companies. They make an investment in the company and have a stake in its success because they become part owners of it.

A company can also borrow money from a commercial bank. It can sell bonds to investors through an investment banker. Bond sales would raise money and a company would gain more visibility, but they represent long-term debt for the company. An established company might issue *commercial paper*—corporate IOUs that are due after 30 to 90 days. Except for venture-capital funding, with each of these choices, the company must pay interest, thereby depleting its resources.

Issuing Stock Another way for a company to raise money is to issue and sell stock. Stock does not represent debt for the company but rather ownership of the company by the shareholders who bought the stock. A public offering of stock will bring in a large infusion of cash.

Internal Financing Another way to fund growth is with money generated from the business itself. The company's profits are plowed back into the business in order to expand operations. This is known as *internal financing*, and it is the best way to fund a company's growth over a long period of time. (See pages 16 and 17.)

HOW DO GROWTH STOCKS GROW?

Growth stocks grow in two interconnected ways: in value and over time. When a company expands production of its products or services and thereby increases its earnings, it becomes worth more overall. The company's stock then becomes more valuable and thereby more attractive to investors. As more investors buy the stock, its price is driven up. If the company continues to grow, the price of the stock will increase, as well.

As a company expands, its growth shows up to shareholders in certain ways over time. This is apparent through the benefits discussed in the following sections.

Stock Dividends Many small growth companies do not pay out large dividends, but over a period of time an investor in the company can receive a large annual dividend check. Dividends are paid out when the company is prosperous and does not need to retain most of its earnings for

THE ADVANTAGES OF INTERNAL FINANCING

Internal financing is a favored method for funding a company's growth. With this technique, a company retains a large part of its earnings and plows the money back into the business, rather than paying it out in dividends.

The table at right compares three companies that have differing financial policies. The three companies are NewCo Inc., Lot O' Gro' Co., and Hidiv Corp. The table shows how the equity, or net worth, of the companies grew over a period of three years, 1985–1987.

Stock in NewCo Inc. was sold to the public for the first time in 1984. To help the company grow, NewCo's management decided not to pay out any dividends to its shareholders. Lot O' Gro' Co. was an older company that was still growing rapidly. It retained 75 percent of its earnings but paid the other 25 percent out in dividends. The third company, Hidiv Corp., was a relatively young organization trying to attract shareholders by paying out large annual dividends, keeping only 30 percent of earnings to fuel its growth.

Assume that each company began in 1985 with $100 million in equity, had a net income (income minus expenses and taxes) of $25 million that year, and that the net incomes of each company increased 20 percent in each of the next two years.

The table starts with the 1985 net income of each company, or $25 million (line 1). Dividends are subtracted (line 2) to give the amount of money that each company retained (line 3). Then, the amount of money ($100 million) with which each company started in January 1985 (known as year-end equity for the preceding year) is added (line 4). Line 5 shows the resulting net worth of each company for 1985. The same process is repeated for 1986 (lines 6–10) and 1987 (lines 11–15). In each year, NewCo retained all earnings, and after three years they showed equity of $191 million. Lot O' Gro' paid out 25 percent of earnings and ended the period with $168 million in equity. Meanwhile, Hidiv paid out 70 percent of earnings and had an equity of only $127 million.

The summary at the bottom of the table shows how much equity each company started with and how much each had after three years. It also lists the percentage of growth in equity that each company attained. NewCo Inc., by retaining all of its earnings, almost doubled its equity in three years, whereas Hidiv Corp. grew by little more than 27 percent. After three years, NewCo Inc., was worth more. The price of its stock probably reflected its increased value. And it had more money than the other two companies to spend on expanding its operations.

		NewCo Inc. 0% Dividend Payout	Lot O' Gro' Co. 25% Dividend Payout	Hidiv Corp. 70% Dividend Payout
1.	Net Income 1985	$ 25,000,000	$ 25,000,000	$ 25,000,000
2.	Dividends Paid Out	− 0	− 6,250,000	− 17,500,000
3.	Retained Earnings	25,000,000	18,750,000	7,500,000
4.	Year-End 1984 Equity	+ 100,000,000	+ 100,000,000	+ 100,000,000
5.	Year-End 1985 Equity	125,000,000	118,750,000	107,500,000
6.	Net Income 1986	$ 30,000,000	$ 30,000,000	$ 30,000,000
7.	Dividends Paid Out	− 0	− 7,500,000	− 21,000,000
8.	Retained Earnings	$ 30,000,000	22,500,000	9,000,000
9.	Year-End 1985 Equity	+ 125,000,000	+ 118,750,000	+ 107,500,000
10.	Year-End 1986 Equity	155,000,000	141,250,000	116,500,000
11.	Net Income 1987	$ 36,000,000	$ 36,000,000	$ 36,000,000
12.	Dividends Paid Out	− 0	− 9,000,000	− 25,200,000
13.	Retained Earnings	36,000,000	27,000,000	10,800,000
14.	Year-End 1986 Equity	+ 155,000,000	+ 141,250,000	+ 116,500,000
15.	Year-End 1987 Equity	191,000,000	108,250,000	127,300,000

Three-Year Summary

	NewCo Inc.	Lot O' Gro' Co.	Hidiv Corp.
Beginning Equity	$100,000,000	$100,000,000	$100,000,000
Ending Equity	191,000,000	168,250,000	127,300,000
Monetary Growth	91,000,000	68,250,000	27,300,000
Percentage Growth	91.00%	68.25%	27.30%

IBM's Selective Sequence Electronic Calculator, introduced in 1947. This early computer system was one in a long progression that advanced the company and the computer industry. It was IBM's first stored program machine, able to hold in its memory instructions for the calculations it was to perform.

funding its growth. Investors who bought IBM stock in 1953, for example, today receive a dividend check that is larger than their entire original investment.

Stock Splits Growth stocks usually multiply over time. When a company has grown and prospered, its management may decide on a *stock split*, which increases the number of shares outstanding without changing the total monetary value of the company's stock. In a three-for-one stock split, for example, a company will replace an investor's 100 shares, each worth $3, with 300 shares of new stock, each now worth $1, but the overall value of the stockholder's investment will be the same—$300. Companies will decide to split their outstanding shares when the per-share price gets too high for investors. Different companies have different ideas about what price is too high. Many try to keep prices below $70 per share, while others happily break the $100 barrier.

For the investor, repeated stock splits can turn an original purchase into a substantial number of shares. For example, a purchase of 100 shares of IBM stock in 1914, when Thomas J. Watson, Sr., was hired to run the small, obscure company, would have grown to 296,600 shares by 1979, when the company split its stock for the thirteenth time.

Resale Value When shareholders of a growth stock decide to sell their stock after a period of time, they will receive more money for the shares at the time of resale. This is because the company's shares are desirable to other investors, and they will pay a high price for them.

IDENTIFYING GROWTH STOCKS

Investment-industry professionals identify growth stocks by analyzing specific industries and companies. An investor can read of their findings in the financial pages of newspapers and in various business publications. Using such publications, an investor can follow a company, see how the experts evaluate its growth potential, and then compare it to that of other companies.

Several sources such as Standard & Poor's Corporation, Merrill Lynch and other brokerage firms, and various financial publications publish lists of growth companies and stocks. For example, the charts on pages 20 and 21 list the top 100 growth companies for 1987 according to *Financial World* magazine. The magazine analyzed large and small growth companies, and its full listing points out the 250 fastest-growing companies in each category. The average growth rate, as measured by earnings per share, for the larger companies over the 3 to 5 years prior to 1987 was 74 percent; for the smaller ones, 65 percent. However, to illustrate how rapidly a successful company can grow, Triangle Industries, the top growth company in all categories, grew 375 percent over the same time period. The potential for capital appreciation with this stock is great.

Analysts use a variety of criteria to identify growth stocks, but they may not all assign the same value to each of their measures in their analysis. Also, their selections represent the judgment or opinion of each group of analysts, and there is no guarantee that investing in any one of the growth stocks on any list will result in dramatic success. Therefore, individual investors should always compare several listings and do some of their own research and analysis before buying a specific stock.

TOP GROWTH COMPANIES

Above $100 Million In Sales

Rank	Company	Trailing 3-5 Yr. EPS[1] (%)	Trailing 12-Mo. EPS ($)	Return on Total Capital[2] (%)	Trailing 12-Mo. Sales ($ mil)	Recent Price ($)	P/E Ratio
1	Triangle Industries	375	2.67	4.13	3,096.1	36.00	13
2	Reebok Intl.	238	2.75	43.57	1,031.9	42.25	15
3	Catalyst Energy	226	0.76	5.98	309.5	21.25	28
4	Allegheny & West'n Energy	224	2.29	14.31	227.1	28.75	13
5	NV Ryan L P	214	0.81	43.53	380.0	9.00	11
6	Minnetonka	179	0.60	22.31	182.6	16.50	28
7	Jewelcor	162	2.40	5.25	244.2	15.25	6
8	3Com	156	0.76	19.98	110.4	18.50	24
9	Best Buy	152	0.98	25.26	239.5	14.75	15
10	UCCEL	151	1.09	9.14	150.3	41.25	38
11	Thermo Electron	141	0.87	6.55	346.6	23.13	27
12	Circle Express	140	0.65	6.15	158.3	10.75	17
13	Toro	137	1.49	15.41	496.1	19.50	13
14	MMR Holding	130	1.12	22.13	236.0	21.00	19
15	U.S. Healthcare	126	1.49	40.03	547.8	13.38	9
16	Wyse Technology	122	1.50	16.41	260.0	26.63	18
17	Pilgrim's Pride	120	1.00	13.87	413.4	9.25	9
18	Healthcare Int'l Cl A	118	0.64	2.44	234.9	8.75	14
19	Sun Microsystems	117	1.04	10.57	425.3	40.38	39
20	TSO Financial	117	1.03	7.12	146.3	9.25	9
21	Envirodyne Inds.	112	2.51	7.37	379.5	40.25	16
22	King World Productions	111	0.90	45.29	207.4	27.50	31
23	Hudson Foods Cl A	110	1.53	10.03	337.7	16.75	11
24	Sequa Cl A	110	20.65	17.69	581.4	71.00	3
25	Franklin Resources	109	2.28	53.81	187.2	27.38	12
26	Medco Containment Svcs.	108	0.65	3.55	228.9	36.50	56
27	AST Research	108	1.23	31.39	182.8	14.63	12
28	Manpower	105	1.83	21.05	1,295.3	55.00	30
29	Home Shopping Network	104	0.35	30.43	475.6	18.38	53
30	Trans World Music	101	1.29	21.86	141.7	37.50	29
31	Johnston Industries	100	2.76	18.25	121.3	19.63	7
32	Healthco Intl	100	3.77	5.57	361.8	22.50	6
33	Standard-Pacific L.P.	99	1.13	11.18	319.0	11.63	10
34	Mark IV Industries	97	1.35	2.73	302.9	16.25	12
35	Sequa Cl B	95	19.90	17.69	371.4	74.00	4
36	Genmar Industries	93	0.89	10.97	360.5	12.50	14
37	Calton	92	0.85	9.05	141.6	9.13	11
38	Ashton-Tate	92	1.39	28.51	229.8	25.00	18
39	Harleysville Group	91	1.53	7.29	166.0	16.25	11
40	COMPAQ Computer	89	1.78	12.57	692.2	44.38	25
41	Courier	89	2.22	9.04	129.6	19.75	9
42	WTD Industries	87	0.86	20.02	176.2	20.88	24
43	Lionel	87	0.61	27.04	297.0	8.38	14
44	Clothes Time	84	0.88	43.95	170.1	22.25	25
45	Harman Int'l Industries	84	1.76	22.04	300.6	15.50	9
46	Willcox & Gibbs	84	1.16	9.14	276.1	21.38	18
47	Oracle Systems	83	0.36	17.21	101.7	21.00	58
48	Beeba's Creations	82	0.89	12.51	101.7	14.25	16
49	Chrysler Holding	82	5.98	24.92	23,261.5	34.63	6
50	Singer	82	3.01	9.53	1,782.5	38.63	13

1. Compounded annual EPS growth rate. 2. Income divided by shareholder equity plus long term debt.

Sources: William O'Neil & Co., Inc. and Vestek Systems, Inc.

TOP GROWTH COMPANIES

Below $100 Million In Sales

Rank	Company	Trailing 3-5 Yr. EPS[1] (%)	Trailing 12-Mo. EPS ($)	Return on Total Capital[2] (%)	Trailing 12-Mo. Sales ($ mil)	Recent Price ($)	P/E Ratio
1	Rockwood National	234	0.51	15.11	19.1	3.69	7
2	Trust America Service	197	1.13	64.65	9.9	16.25	14
3	Northeastern Mtge.	190	0.82	NC	29.4	7.75	9
4	Autodesk	181	0.61	30.56	58.7	20.75	34
5	Warner Computer Sys.	179	0.29	28.19	18.6	6.75	23
6	AMRE	164	0.30	42.45	65.4	16.13	54
7	General Magnaplate	162	0.60	8.76	6.8	5.75	10
8	New Line Cinema	158	1.14	30.11	36.0	7.25	6
9	Perception Technology	156	0.27	7.59	14.7	17.50	65
10	Riedel Environmental Tech.	148	0.43	30.57	35.9	23.63	55
11	EMC Corp Mass	139	1.26	25.34	75.9	28.50	23
12	Mayfair Industries	138	0.73	2.57	26.9	11.25	15
13	Polymeric Resources	132	0.31	3.09	14.4	3.75	12
14	Computrac	129	0.29	21.02	10.1	7.75	27
15	Brock Exploration	127	0.27	9.85	7.4	2.25	8
16	Coated Sales	121	0.40	16.51	90.0	11.88	30
17	Dual Lite	120	1.83	19.00	41.0	25.75	14
18	Matthews & Wright Group	116	1.93	30.03	42.6	3.13	2
19	Insituform North America	115	0.34	10.00	14.0	16.63	49
20	Sigma Designs	115	0.71	40.93	34.7	14.25	20
21	Jiffy Lube Int'l	114	0.30	2.05	44.2	14.63	49
22	Barris Industries	114	1.86	19.52	61.9	14.63	8
23	V Band	113	1.06	19.99	45.3	27.75	26
24	Rotech Medical	113	0.16	14.90	10.8	5.75	36
25	NEECO	111	0.70	60.80	59.3	18.00	26
26	CareerCom	111	0.44	16.43	51.0	8.88	20
27	United Insurance	111	1.97	10.68	85.6	18.00	9
28	Beauticontrol Cosmetics	109	0.71	24.03	23.4	7.25	10
29	Barry's Jewelers	108	0.69	4.66	83.7	7.88	11
30	TCBY Enterprises	104	0.40	18.50	40.9	13.75	39
31	Nord Resources	104	1.01	15.48	63.4	16.75	17
32	Merrill Corp.	104	0.69	12.16	51.0	14.00	20
33	Howell Industries	103	2.90	12.99	50.4	31.75	11
34	Atalanta/Sosnoff Cap.	102	1.03	15.95	33.4	11.63	11
35	SunGard Data Systems	102	0.66	20.11	75.0	18.25	28
36	Brandon Systems	102	0.72	42.43	19.5	11.75	16
37	Tech Data	101	0.56	16.80	92.5	11.00	20
38	ALZA C1 A	100	0.31	7.27	56.0	37.50	121
39	Reeds Jewelers	100	0.59	28.09	34.8	7.50	13
40	System Software Assoc.	100	0.50	35.10	20.1	17.00	34
41	Ben & Jerry's Homemade	99	0.70	6.94	21.7	23.50	34
42	Reich & Tang L.P.	99	1.41	348.44	32.6	14.75	10
43	HDR Power Systems	98	0.56	441.34	8.4	5.00	9
44	Iverson Technology	97	0.63	25.49	25.0	13.25	21
45	Durakon Industries	96	0.78	12.51	88.1	11.63	15
46	Daylight Industries	93	0.13	14.48	0.8	3.75	29
47	Telos	92	0.71	34.59	78.8	8.75	12
48	Moore-Handley	91	0.45	3.02	88.3	8.00	18
49	Polk Audio	91	0.58	45.25	16.8	8.50	15
50	Actmedia	90	0.46	9.95	72.9	26.88	58

Sources: William O'Neil & Co., Inc., and Vestek Systems, Inc.

1. Compounded annual EPS growth rate. 2. Income divided by shareholder equity plus long term debt.

A technician enters data onto a Cray Super 2 Computer from a work station. Cray Research, Inc., is the world's leading developer of supercomputers, machines that can perform hundreds of millions of operations per second.

Identifying Growth Industries

The first step in choosing a growth stock is to identify industries that are expanding. Investors can begin to do this by taking note of what products their friends frequently buy or what services they often use. In the 1970s, fast food became popular, and its industry quickly turned into a growth industry. Industries expanding in the 1980s included health and exercise clubs, sports clothing, electronics items such as videocassette recorders (VCRs) and compact disk recordings (CDs), and, of course, almost anything relating to computers.

At any given time, an industry that is being bolstered by ongoing technological advances within its field is likely to be expanding. For example, the computer industry in the 1980s is a growth industry, as opposed to the steel industry. Cray Research, although no longer a new computer company, still has a strong potential for growth because of the incredible capabilities of the supercomputers it manufactures. The company's computers are used for such complicated jobs as weather forecasting and missile tracking. Investors are likely to find spectacular growth in industries that have made new breakthroughs in technology.

Another way to discover where there are growth trends in industries is to follow industry news. The financial pages of newspapers, business magazines, and industry journals include information on various industries. They report the introduction of new products, technological advances in a certain field, and the creation of new companies. Some even feature articles on specific growth industries.

The classified ads of a newspaper can also offer information on what industries are growing. By following job opportunities over a period of time, an investor can determine in what areas there is expansion.

After a 156-day voyage, the barge Mobro *docks in Brooklyn to unload unwanted garbage in August 1987. The partnership that owned the garbage hoped to recycle it and turn it into fuel. Because of the problem of increased refuse in the United States, waste disposal is becoming a growth industry.*

Identifying Growth Companies

Every company in a growth industry is a growth company, but some companies will prove better than others at sustaining high growth. Such companies share three basic characteristics. Investment-industry professionals and investors seeking opportunities in growth stocks should look for all three of them in a company.

Demand for a Product or Service A good growth company must have a product or service in high and continuous demand by customers. There are several possible reasons why a product may be in demand.

Often a company is a leader in its industry because its products or services are highly distinct, if not unique. Waste-Management is a company that offers a distinct service; it specializes in garbage and hazardous-waste disposal. The company developed a commanding position in its industry after it had acquired dozens of disposal sites all over the country. Because of the enormous difficulty of establishing new sites, prospective competitors were at a major disadvantage.

Edwin H. Land, founder of the Polaroid Corporation, demonstrates his company's innovative one-step photography to the public for the first time in February 1947. Polaroid is one of the best examples of a growth company. Between 1957 and 1969, its stock rose from $5 to $145 per share.

Some company's products or services may be in great demand because the company has a technological lead over others in its field. Digital Equipment Corporation, for instance, provides minicomputers that have superior communications capabilities.

There is also a strong and predictable demand for products that are patented and have no competition. Drug and pharmaceutical companies often achieve high levels of growth when a patented product becomes a best-seller. Syntex Corp., for example, has a brand of anti-inflammatory medication used to control the pain of arthritis. Naprosyn became one of the best-selling drugs in the United States in the mid-1980s. When the Polaroid Corporation introduced its Land camera in 1948 it became an immediate success. The camera produced instant photographs, and nothing like it existed on the market. The company patented its product, and today the camera is still free of competition in its field.

When a company is a leader in its industry, it can maintain relatively high prices for a product or service that is recognized and in demand. If the company had to lower its prices in order to attract customers, it would not be able to increase its sales, the profits from which are essential for furthering the growth of a company.

Competent Management A second characteristic of a growth company is that it has an imaginative and competent management team that is guided by established company goals. The managers compose a team of people who lead and coordinate all of the activities and employees of a company so that it can achieve its production and sales goals. Some managers work with people outside the company, such as suppliers. Others make plans for the future of the company. Some components of good management are strength in production, marketing, good customer and employee relations, and strong community ties.

A growth company should have a well-developed marketing program to promote its product or service. Without wide and continued exposure to consumers, a product cannot sell, which ultimately means that demand for the product and profits from its sales will diminish.

To help ensure that customers continue to buy a product or service, a company must follow up on its sales and offer good service to its customers. Consumers will respond to such efforts by remaining loyal to the company and by promoting its product to others.

Management not only coordinates customer relations but is also responsible for seeing that a company has a stable work force. In order to do so, the company must have good employee relations. This is expressed in various ways, such as in benefits to employees and in ongoing communication about what is happening within the company.

Encouraging the creativity and participation of employees can lead to new product ideas or improved procedures. An employee of 3M was the inventor of one of its most popular office supplies: self-sticking, precut notepapers that are removable and reusable.

Some companies offer such benefits as training and incentive programs as well as flexible work hours. These kinds of programs can increase productivity. Others offer day care for employees' children and athletic facilities to their employees.

Employee relations are important because, when the people working at a company are satisfied with their work conditions and have a positive attitude toward their employer, they are likely to be more productive.

The management of a company must be aware of how society and the environment are being affected by the company's products. Ultimately it is good business for the company to take a responsible position and offer or manufacture products that help consumers in some way and are ecologically safe.

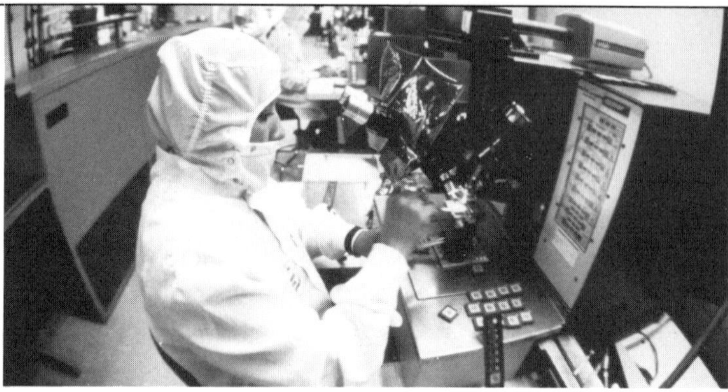

Technicians assemble 32-bit computer chips at a Motorola plant. These chips, which are used in advanced personal computers of the late 1980s, contain twice as many miniaturized electrical circuits as the previous generation of chips.

Research and Development The last important element of a growth company is that it puts a large part of its earnings into a high-quality research and development (R & D) program. Companies must experiment with new product ideas. The various people who are hired to do this make up an R & D team.

Researchers are employees who think up innovative ideas for possible products or services. They must first investigate what customers want or might be interested in. When a researcher comes up with an idea for a potentially successful product, that idea has to be developed. The other members of the R & D team explore and experiment with the idea and turn it into an actual product or service. Then it is further perfected.

Being able to continually offer new or improved products to the public is important for guaranteeing future incoming capital. This has been especially important in the drug, computer, and electronics fields.

USING STATISTICS TO ANALYZE A COMPANY

In addition to looking at the products, management, and research programs of a company, its statistics must also be reviewed. Statistical analysis of the past and present financial conditions of a company is an essential element in identifying growth situations. Financial analysts have developed various tools for judging a company's condition. These growth-rate calculations and measurements of profitability are especially useful when comparing companies operating in the same industry or with similar characteristics.

The financial section of a company's annual report provides the data used by analysts to evaluate companies. Individual investors can request annual reports from companies in which they are interested.

The three elements of the financial section that provide this data are the income statement, the balance sheet, and the source and application of funds statement. The income statement provides a history of a company's sales, costs, and tax payments for the past year. The balance sheet shows what a company owns, what it owes, and its overall value. The source and application of funds statement, also known as a cash flow statement, explains how the company's financial position changed in the past year. What follows is a description of the tools used for analysis.

EPS For a company to be a good growth-stock investment, it must show a record of growth in earnings over the last 5 to 10 years as well as stable or improving profits. A company's *earnings per share (EPS)* is one of the most fundamental measures used in security analysis.

EPS is calculated by dividing a company's profits, or *net income*, by the number of shares outstanding, the shares of stock owned by investors. Because investors buy or sell stocks based on the price of an individual share, analysts find it useful to see how much of a company's earnings each share commands. By studying data on past earnings per share, an investor can assess what future earnings may be like.

ROE A company's *return on equity (ROE)* is another measure of profitability. ROE is a ratio (normally expressed as a percentage) that shows the relationship between a company's net income and its *stockholders' equity*, or their investment interest in the company. Stockholders' equity is the amount that remains after a company's liabilities (debts) have been subtracted from its assets. It can be found in the balance sheet. Financial analysts consider a company's ROE to be the best measure of its profitability. The ROE indicates the rate of investment return the managers of the company have been able to obtain with the stockholders' money. For an established growth company, 25 percent returns are not uncommon.

Reinvestment Rate A growth company worth investing in should be able to finance most or all of its future growth internally. To determine whether this type of funding is possible, a company must evaluate its internal growth rate, or income *reinvestment rate*. The rate is determined by multiplying a company's ROE by its *income retention rate*.

The income retention rate is the percentage of a company's earnings that is reinvested into the business rather than paid out in dividends to investors. The reinvestment rate should be high, or it should show prospects of a higher rate in the future.

To calculate a company's reinvestment rate, assume, for example, that it has a ROE of 16 percent, earns $4 per share, and pays an annual dividend of $1 per share. Then:

$$\text{Reinvestment Rate} = \text{Return on Equity} \times \text{Retention Rate}$$

$$\text{Potential Internal Growth Rate} = 16\% \times \frac{\$4.00-\$1.00}{\$4.00}$$

$$12\% = 16\% \times 75\%$$

The result shows that unless this company improves its ROE by increasing profits or pays out less to its stockholders each year, it could not grow faster than 12 percent per year. In comparison with some growth companies of the 1980s, this is not a high rate.

Using the reinvestment-rate formula is a way of determining a company's ability to internally finance, but it should be used with care by a potential investor who is analyzing the company. A low-quality company can achieve a high ROE if stockholders' equity is small in relation to profits, which could be the result of several unprofitable years. When a company's return on equity and return on assets are both high, the reinvestment-rate formula can be used with greater confidence.

P/E Ratio A company's *price/earnings (P/E) ratio* is another important tool for analyzing a stock's potential. It is calculated by dividing the company's annual earnings by its stock price. For example, if a company's stock is selling for $30 and its latest earnings were $1.50 a share, its P/E ratio is 20. This means that its share price is 20 times its earnings per share.

Use of the P/E ratio is a convenient way to relate a stock's price to its earnings. It can also reveal something about investor expectations. A very high P/E may mean that a company's stock price has been raised by numerous investors who bought it in the belief that the company's future is very rosy. These stocks should be analyzed carefully to see whether they have become overpriced in view of the company's actual earnings potential. Because growth stocks often have high P/Es, investors should study these companies especially carefully to see whether their prospects for future earnings are already reflected in their stock price.

Liability In addition to the financial tools listed above, analysts review a company's *liabilities*. These are its debts, or what the company owes. The balance sheet divides debt into short- and long-term debt. Short-term debt is what is owed within the next 12 months. It includes such payments as those to suppliers. Long-term debt is to be paid back sometime after the next year. Bonds are listed under this category. A good growth company maintains a conservative amount of debt so that it can reinvest its earnings in the company and not have to use them to pay off debt each year.

A customer shopping at Sears. When it was founded, Sears Roebuck & Company was a growth company. Today its stock is considered a reliable blue chip.

LEARNING FROM THE PAST

The rewards of investing in growing companies can be great, but to reap those rewards investors must select the right stock and be patient while the company, and its stock's value, grows. Tracking the successful and unsuccessful growth companies of the past and looking at the industries in which they operated can help today's investors choose companies with growth potential.

Investors must remember, however, that the successful growth stocks of today will become the mature blue chips of tomorrow, to be replaced by a new generation of growth stocks. In every decade of the 20th century, new industries have sprung up. With continuing advances in technology, more will evolve, creating new and different growth industries. The growth stocks of the 1920s were in the automobile, chemical, motion-picture, and radio industries. In the 1940s and 1950s they were in such industries as consumer appliances and self-service centers such as laundromats. A decade later, growth-stock investors were putting their money in the field of electronics, office equipment, health services, cosmetics, and specialty publishing, among others.

It is important for prospective investors to know about recent industry trends and also to learn from the past performance of some industries that did not live up to expectations.

Recent Eras of Investing

There have been several distinct eras of growth-stock investing in the postwar period that began in 1945. Between 1950 and 1973, a few growth stocks were in particular demand by the managers of huge stock portfolios, such as pension and mutual funds. Institutional purchases of these growth stocks—which included Avon Products, Xerox, and Polaroid—pushed their prices and their P/E ratios to an extremely high level. Small investors, seeing the activity, were eager to buy in, too.

Meanwhile, the many less glamorous stocks on the market suffered neglect by comparison. With less dramatic increases in their prices, there was less investor activity, and their P/Es were modest. Stock market authorities began to talk about a two-tier market, calling the growth stocks in the top tier "the nifty 50."

This era ended for all practical purposes in late 1973, when OPEC, the organization of oil-producing countries, for foreign policy reasons, halted the exportation of oil to the United States. The oil embargo reduced the supply of fuel, limiting industrial expansion and reducing consumption of goods already on the market. For the rest of the 1970s, the economy, the stock market, and the American people themselves grappled in different ways with "stagflation"—little or no industrial growth, stagnant consumer demand, and high rates of inflation and unemployment. Between about 1970 and 1982, the rate of inflation rose to double-digit (percentage rate of 10 or more) levels. The purchasing power of the dollar declined, almost wiping out the investment returns on common stocks for many investors.

By 1982 inflation had subsided, but investors did not fully realize the change at first. The Dow Jones Industrial Average, a stock market index consisting of the stock prices

THE MOVIES AS A GROWTH INDUSTRY

The motion picture industry is an old, established industry, but one that has, since its beginning in the early 20th century, always been characterized by volatility and unpredictability. However, the movie industry has been a growth industry and, even when not in a long-term growth period, has experienced tremendous expansion. Growth has occurred when technological advances attracted large audiences to the movies. Between the bursts of growth, however, the film industry has experienced major slumps.

By the time World War I began in 1914, the movies were a popular form of entertainment. Early films lacked color and sound (although they were often accompanied by a live pianist in the theater). Subtitles flashed on the screen between the scenes provided the dialogue. During that war the silent film comedy was developed, characterized by silly, slapstick humor. Charlie Chaplin, Buster Keaton, and others became box-office favorites in these comedies, bringing increased profits to film studios and helping to make the movie industry a growth industry in the postwar 1920s.

By then the film industry had become big business. Small independent studios turned into large corporations that produced, marketed, and exhibited films. In 1919 Paramount Pictures had become the first movie company to issue stock to the public.

Charlie Chaplin in The Gold Rush, *one of the great silent film comedies of the mid-1920s. By this point the movie industry had become a growth industry.*

In the late 1920s, movie industry growth slowed in the face of competition from radio and the automobile, which offered other forms of entertainment. Attendance at movie theaters declined. One production studio, Warner Brothers, was having particular financial difficulties. It decided to take a gamble on a screen version of a popular play, *The Jazz Singer*, using a new process called Vitaphone to introduce recorded songs to the movie. During production, a few lines ad-libbed after a song by actor Al Jolson were mistakenly recorded. The spoken word sounded as good as the singing, prompting Warner to record some more dialogue for the film. The first talking feature movie was born.

When *The Jazz Singer* premiered on October 6, 1927, it was an immediate success. Every major studio converted to sound as rapidly as possible. The movie industry became even more of a booming growth industry and high stock prices reflected that growth.

The popularity of the new movies carried the film industry through the first

Al Jolson and Eugenie Besserer in The Jazz Singer, *the first movie to include spoken dialogue as well as songs. Released in 1927, it marked the end of the silent film era.*

years of the Great Depression, which began in 1929. During this period of hard times, the movies provided an escape. Wall Street firms called the movies a depression-proof industry. By 1931, however, the industry had succumbed to national economic problems and slumped. But then new technology brought color to feature films. The first Technicolor film was *Becky Sharp*, presented in 1935. It was followed by such other landmark films as *A Star Is Born* (1937), *Gone with the Wind* (1939), and *The Wizard of Oz* (1939). All were extremely popular, and movie-company stock prices rose again until the late 1940s.

Then television began to threaten the industry. In 1952 the entire United States gained access to network television. As more and more people began watching the small black-and-white screens in their living rooms, movie theater attendance went down. The industry tried new gimmicks to recapture its audiences: wide screens, stereophonic sound, and efforts to achieve three-dimensional effects. But attendance still declined. Theaters around the country were closing down.

The 1960s and early 1970s saw an overall slump in the movie industry as it went through a period of transition. Film studio stock prices trailed general stock market prices during this time.

Then, in the late 1970s movie producers and art directors had a new technology to explore: computers that could create special effects. *Star Wars*, written and directed by George Lucas in 1977, was one of the first movies with computer-generated effects. The movie broke ticket sales records. In a string of successes—*E.T.*, *Close Encounters of the Third Kind*, *Raiders of the Lost Ark*, and *Aliens*, among others—the new technology brought audiences of all ages back to movie theaters. Film studio stock prices steadily rose above overall stock market prices. In the 1980s, the movie industry is growing again.

Mark Hamill, Alec Guinness, and Harrison Ford in Star Wars. *The special effects were the main reason for the movie's tremendous popularity in 1977.*

A sign of the Arab oil embargo of 1973: Cars wind around a New York City block while their drivers wait to fill up their tanks at the station. Gas was at a premium because the members of OPEC had cut off the exportation of oil to the United States.

of 30 large companies, had topped 1,000 points for the first time 10 years earlier. In August 1982 the Dow hit its lowest point in more than 2 years when it closed at 776.9. A few days later, after a well-known Wall Street economist predicted that interest rates on bank loans would continue to fall, the Dow jumped a record 38 points. Investors began to anticipate an expanding national economy. A third era, the great bull market (rising stock prices) of the 1980s, had begun. The Dow reached 1,100 in 1983. It ebbed at certain points but still went tirelessly up. Four years later, in August 1987, the market went to more than 2,700 for the first time. When the Dow plunged to 1,783 two months later, the causes of the decline were not immediately apparent, but the risks of investing in stocks were.

Risks in Growth-Stock Investing

Investors must be aware that they are taking a risk when they make an investment in a growth stock. A growth-stock investor is betting on the future of a company. Sometimes the investor does not accurately predict the future growth of a company and its stock. At other times, a stock does not fulfill its promise.

There are many reasons why a company may not grow as expected. It could be that a competing company develops a product that is technologically more advanced or that a new company takes business away from it. Sometimes it is because another company takes it over. Another possibility is that the cost of materials grows too high.

Growth-stock investors have to be wary of investment fads (favorites of the day), as well. Sometimes a particular stock or group of stocks can become very popular in the investment world. As stock prices increase, more people put money into the stocks with the hope of making greater capital gains. Such stocks may flourish for one or two years, allowing participants to resemble true growth companies. But then the industry declines, or the company's earnings decrease, and stock prices fall rapidly.

Examples of some short-lived growth industries of the past include exercise clubs and boating in the late 1950s; bowling and certain electronics businesses in the early 1960s; computer leasing in the late 1960s; warehouse merchandising in the early 1970s; and TV merchandising in the late 1980s. Many investors ultimately lost money when they bought stock from companies in these industries and then the stock either did not increase in value or its price declined because of lack of product demand.

It may be difficult to distinguish between an investment fad and an obscure but emerging growth stock. Investors should make an effort to learn about the weaknesses as well as the strengths of the industry, acquire an understanding of the economics of the business, and maintain a long-term perspective. They should have confidence that the market for the company's or industry's products or services is expanding and is not just temporary. A company with a group of related products, for example, will be better cushioned against an event that can adversely affect the market for one of its products.

Excited traders on the floor of the New York Stock Exchange on a day of record sales. During the mid-1980s the stock market rose steadily.

THE UPS AND DOWNS OF THE COMPUTER INDUSTRY

In the early years of the 1980s bull market, investors in small, emerging growth companies focused a lot of attention on high-tech stocks, the stocks from companies that are involved in manufacturing highly complex scientific products and components. Their interest was stimulated by the early popularity of the personal computer, or microcomputer. Apple Computer Co. and two products called VisiCalc and Lotus 1-2-3 played an important role in introducing small computers to American homes and businesses. Their story helps illustrate why investing in some growth stocks is risky.

Apple's model II computer, first sold in 1977, was one of the earliest personal computers. At first only hobbyists bought Apple computers. At that time, there were few functions that most people could perform with a computer. Each owner had to give the computer specific instructions by writing a program. Furthermore, the computers had only limited memory and therefore could not "remember" many instructions or facts simultaneously. Although at the time there were many optimistic predictions for the future of personal computing, in reality there were few computers on the market and little for them to do. Then Software Arts Inc., which was developing prepared programs for computers, or software, introduced a business product called VisiCalc. The product was an electronic spreadsheet. It allowed bookkeepers, accountants, business managers, and other "number-crunching" professionals to do much of their mathematical work on a computer instead of with paper, pencil, and a calculator.

For a while, Apple was in a very enviable position. Its computer was in great demand. For one thing, few companies made personal computers. More important, however, many people wanted to buy an Apple computer because VisiCalc had been designed to work on it; VisiCalc could not operate on any other personal computer. The company improved its computer, developing other models with more memory. Other companies offered additional software packages, turning the personal computer into a flexible machine with an ever-growing market. Apple's stock rose to a high of $63 per share in 1983.

Apple's luck was too good to last. Before long, the young computer company began to face strong competition. IBM, the largest computer company in the world, introduced its own personal computer, the IBM PC. New versions of VisiCalc were developed to work not just on an Apple but on other personal computers, as well. Finally, a new company called Lotus Development Corporation introduced a software package in the fall of 1982, Lotus 1-2-3. Lotus did the same things as VisiCalc but considerably better. It was the first integrated software package, combining simple word processing and graphics with a spreadsheet. Users could write reports to go with their financial tables and illustrate them with graphs. Lotus 1-2-3 was designed to work on the IBM PC, not on an Apple.

The introduction of Lotus 1-2-3 gave IBM's PC a competitive edge—a serious blow to both Apple and VisiCalc. Everything Apple and VisiCalc did, IBM and Lotus did better. The first electronic spreadsheet program became outdated almost overnight, and Apple was superseded in the business world. Apple's stock price fell dramatically. In 1985 it reached a low of $14. The company had a difficult year as it tried to stabilize by tightening operations and developing new products. It was able to boost its profits substantially by introducing to the market its innovative Macintosh computer and targeting the educational and home computer markets for its smaller machines. In 1986, Apple earned $154 million on sales of $1.9 billion and successfully reemerged as a growth company.

Meanwhile, Lotus Development had gone public in 1983 and was an instant success. For a few years the company had spectacular growth as sales went from almost zero to $282.2 million in 1986. Profits that year were $48.3 million, a 27 percent increase over the previous year, and Lotus dominated the electronic spreadsheet market. Nevertheless, financial analysts, wondering whether the company could continue to grow at this rapid rate, felt that the market was saturated. Everyone who needed a spreadsheet program had already bought Lotus 1-2-3. Opinions differed as to whether Lotus was a "one-product company" or a genuine growth company that would have above-average growth over the long term.

Apple, VisiCalc, IBM, Lotus, and a host of other hardware (computers) and software (programs) companies continue to develop new and more advanced products. In October 1987, for example, Microsoft Corporation introduced a spreadsheet program, Excel, designed to work on IBM's advanced Personal System 2 computers.

What will the industry develop next? Nobody knows for sure. The only certainty is that the computer industry will see rapid growth and strong competition for years to come, and that computer-stock prices will continue to go up and down.

AT WHAT PRICE WHEN?

It is one thing to identify a growth stock. Figuring out at what price it should be bought is something else altogether. Wall Street analysts struggle constantly with the questions "How much is a share of this company worth?" and "When should this stock be purchased?" There is no precise answer to these questions. In a broad sense, the best time to buy is before a stock is recognized by the investment market as a growth stock; that is, before its price has been driven too high. Figuring this out is a matter of careful analysis and judgment.

In the short term—a period of days, weeks, or months—the price of any stock will fluctuate within a fairly narrow range. This range usually changes gradually but sometimes suddenly. Over the long term—a year or more—a stock price will usually rise or fall in accord with the company's actual earnings, dividends, and overall financial condition. When a company prospers, it becomes more attractive to investors, and the price of its stock goes up according to the law of supply and demand. This pattern is especially true for growth stocks.

Professionals in the investment world evaluate stock on three levels. Individual investors can also judge whether to buy stocks by considering the following factors:

1. **The Investment Environment** Industry-wide, national, and even international factors constitute the investment environment at any given time. Investors should stay alert to factors that might cause change in the investment environment. The two most important factors are inflation and interest rates.

   Since the 1930s, there has been a steady decline in the purchasing power of the dollar because of inflation. The most dramatic periods of rising inflation were in

1946–47, 1973–74, and the early 1980s. Even the slowdown in the inflation rate in the late 1980s did not halt the long-term trend toward a decline in the dollar. When inflation rates are high, investors will look for greater returns from a stock purchase.

Interest rates are measured by the *prime rate*, the percentage of interest charged by a bank making a loan to its most creditworthy customers. Interest rates remained at a low two to three percent level from 1935 until 1951. Then they climbed gradually through the 1950s to about five percent and maintained that level until around 1966. Since then, the prime rate has risen as high as 18 percent (1981) and fallen as low as 5 percent (1972). When interest rates rise, the cost to companies borrowing money for their operations also rises. Investors then act with caution, because interest paid by a company reduces corporate profits.

Consumer prices have soared since the early 1940s, when ice-cream sundaes cost 25 or 30 cents at this drugstore counter in Zebulon, North Carolina.

2. **Relationship to Other Stocks** Aside from comparing stock prices, the method most frequently used to compare two or more stocks is to compare their P/E ratios (see page 29). The stocks of growth companies usually have higher ratios and lower dividend yields than the stocks of more stable companies. But the same P/E ratio or dividend yield does not mean that stocks will share other characteristics. They may be in different industries with different outlooks and will certainly have different managements. One may be stable and mature, another developing slowly or steadily, and a third growing rapidly. Stock of the company that grows at a faster rate will most likely attract investors' attention and soon should command a higher price in relation to earnings and thus carry a higher P/E ratio.

Securities analysts have devised a variety of formulas throughout history to evaluate individual companies and their growth stocks. For instance, the authors of one financial textbook (*Security Analysis*, David L. Dodd,

Sidney Cottle, and Benjamin Graham, McGraw-Hill, 4th ed., 1962) devised a valuation formula to estimate P/E ratios of companies. The formula was based on historical relationships of P/Es to different interest rates and various long-term (7 to 10 years) growth rates. They used the table seen below to predict P/E ratios and compare actual ratios with the predictions. According to this table, when interest rates are high, a company with a low expected growth rate will have a low P/E ratio. The highest P/E ratios should be obtained by rapid-growth companies in low-interest-rate years (upper left of table). The reasons are clear: When interest rates are low, it costs little for a company to borrow money to fuel its growth. This table does not, however, account for differences between companies growing at the same rate. If the prevailing interest rate is 7 percent, 2 companies with 12 percent growth would both deserve a 20.4 P/E ratio, according to the table. But if one company has a higher ROE and is therefore paying a higher dividend to stockholders, it will probably be

PRICE/EARNINGS RATIOS FOR DIFFERENT GROWTH AND INTEREST RATES

Prevailing Interest Rate

Expected Growth Rate	*3%*	*4%*	*5%*	*6%*	*7%*	*8%*	*9%*	*10%*	*11%*	*12%*	*13%*	*14%*	*15%*	*16%*	*17%*	*18%*
20%	71.2	53.4	42.7	35.6	30.5	26.7	23.7	21.4	19.4	17.8	16.4	15.3	14.2	13.3	12.6	11.9
19%	68.2	51.2	40.9	34.1	29.2	25.6	22.7	20.5	18.6	17.1	15.7	14.6	13.6	12.8	12.0	11.4
18%	65.3	49.0	39.2	32.7	28.0	24.5	21.8	19.6	17.8	16.3	15.1	14.0	13.1	12.2	11.5	10.9
17%	62.4	46.8	37.4	31.2	26.7	23.4	20.8	18.7	17.0	15.6	14.4	13.4	12.5	11.7	11.0	10.4
16%	59.4	44.6	35.7	29.7	25.5	22.3	19.8	17.8	16.2	14.9	13.7	12.7	11.9	11.1	10.5	9.9
15%	56.5	42.4	33.9	28.3	24.2	21.2	18.8	17.0	15.4	14.1	13.0	12.1	11.3	10.6	10.0	9.4
14%	53.6	40.2	32.1	26.8	23.0	20.1	17.9	16.1	14.6	13.4	12.4	11.5	10.7	10.0	9.5	8.9
13%	50.6	38.0	30.4	25.3	21.7	19.0	16.9	15.2	13.8	12.7	11.7	10.9	10.1	9.5	8.9	8.4
12%	47.7	35.8	28.6	23.9	20.4	17.9	15.9	14.3	13.0	11.9	11.0	10.2	9.5	8.9	8.4	8.0
11%	44.8	33.6	26.9	22.4	19.2	16.8	14.9	13.4	12.2	11.2	10.3	9.6	9.0	8.4	7.9	7.5
10%	41.8	31.4	25.1	20.9	17.9	15.7	13.9	12.6	11.4	10.5	9.7	9.0	8.4	7.8	7.4	7.0
9%	38.9	29.2	23.3	19.5	16.7	14.6	13.0	11.7	10.6	9.7	9.0	8.3	7.8	7.3	6.9	6.5
8%	36.0	27.0	21.6	18.0	15.4	13.5	12.0	10.8	9.8	9.0	8.3	7.7	7.2	6.7	6.3	6.0
7%	33.0	24.8	19.8	16.5	14.2	12.4	11.0	9.9	9.0	8.3	7.6	7.1	6.6	6.2	5.8	5.5
6%	30.1	22.6	18.1	15.1	12.9	11.3	10.0	9.0	8.2	7.5	6.9	6.5	6.0	5.6	5.3	5.0
5%	27.2	20.4	16.3	13.6	11.6	10.2	9.1	8.2	7.4	6.8	6.3	5.8	5.4	5.1	4.8	4.5
4%	24.3	18.2	14.5	12.1	10.4	9.1	8.1	7.3	6.6	6.1	5.6	5.2	4.8	4.5	4.3	4.0
3%	21.3	16.0	12.8	10.7	9.1	8.0	7.1	6.4	5.8	5.3	4.9	4.6	4.3	4.0	3.8	3.6

selling at a higher P/E ratio than the predicted 20.4. If it has a low P/E, investors can recognize it as an undervalued company and therefore a good buy.

3. **Individual Merits** An investor must look closely at a stock's price and the situation of the company. The stock tables found in daily newspapers will give a company's current stock price as well as the highest and lowest prices over the last year. Investors should compare past and present stock prices in order to determine whether it is a good time to buy a stock. They have the choice of buying an inexpensive stock and waiting for its price to rise or waiting until a stock's price is definitely climbing and buying it at a higher price.

   An investor should also refer frequently to the stock tables to judge how active a stock has been in the market. If a stock is not trading frequently, it is not in demand and therefore may not be a good current investment.

   A company's financial situation should be strong. If the company is about to borrow money, it may not be a good time to buy its stock. If the company has sophisticated products in great demand and high-quality management, then its stock is probably a good investment. However, companies eventually peak and reach their full potential for development, and investors need to stay alert to when this point has been reached. When companies do peak, their stock will not appreciate as greatly as growth stocks.

   Success in growth-stock investing requires patience, planning, selectivity, and timely information on economic and business trends. Although individual investors can make informed decisions on purchasing growth stocks, most will want to seek the advice of a stockbroker or financial analyst to determine when to buy these stocks.

Employees of Genentech, Inc., monitor conditions for the production of proteins used for medical testing. Biotechnology is a growth industry of the 1980s and beyond.

FUTURE GROWTH STOCKS

What will be the growth stocks of tomorrow? Although it is not possible to be certain, of course, it is possible to make educated guesses. Trends that we can identify in their early stages may give us useful clues. Prospective investors should look for three types of trends: the new directions currently being taken by industries, developments in new industries, and changes taking place in our society.

New Directions in Industries In older, established industries, investors should be alert to new product developments. For instance, satellite transmission and fiber optics represent new technologies that are rapidly changing the telecommunications industry. Voice recognition and response, which allows computers to be activated by spoken commands, is expected to change the computer industry. In the pharmaceutical industry, new drugs from established companies may bring growth. Bristol-Myers, Merck, and Upjohn are producing drugs that lower blood cholesterol levels.

Development in New Industries In every generation there are new industries creating new products and services. One hundred years ago the telephone and typewriter were among the new products. Biotechnology, one relatively new industry of the 1980s, seems to have many growth possibilities. Newspapers tell of numerous research efforts to alter animal and plant life. Laboratory genetics technologies could produce leaner beef, more durable cotton, or drought-resistant crops as well as effective treatments for inherited diseases.

Trends in Society Many changes in the world around us provide opportunities for the development of growth industries. As the two-earner household became commonplace in the 1970s, the fast-food industry flourished—and it continues strong today. What other social trends can be identified? As the 20th century draws to a close, people are living longer. This trend should boost long-term growth of pharmaceutical companies; health-care facilities, such as nursing homes and day-care services for the chronically ill; and appliances, clothing, and transportation adapted for use by the infirm or handicapped.

The keen interest in health that has developed since the 1970s has already translated into growth for health and exercise clubs, clothing and shoes for sports and exercise, exercise equipment, and new food products and stores. Because this trend does not seem to be slowing down, there is still room for growth in many companies.

Today's two-earner households create a demand for new appliances, easy-to-clean materials, easy-to-prepare foods, and products such as microwave ovens that speed up the process of food preparation. The "baby boomlet" of the 1980s created a need for child-care facilities; baby clothing and equipment; school supplies and textbooks; records; movies; and television programs.

To avoid depletion of such natural resources as water, coal, and oil, it is important to explore recycling and the developing of alternatives. There are already water treatment plants, a few buildings using solar energy for some of their needs, and various approaches to turning waste products into energy. We can be sure that the years ahead will see the development of many new growth industries offering products or services that are now perhaps only a gleam in an investor's or entrepreneur's eye.

"TestPacks" (used to diagnose streptococcal infections) manufactured by Abbott Laboratories. Development of new medications and use of advanced technology will make pharmaceutical companies growth industries well into the 21st century.

GLOSSARY

assets Everything that a company owns, including what is owed to it. Assets can include cash, equipment, or patents.

bear market A market in which stock prices are consistently falling.

blue chip stocks (blue chips) Stocks issued by companies that are noted for their financial stability and ability to maintain earnings and make high dividend payments.

bond A certificate that represents a loan to a company or government agency. The issuing company (the borrower) pays interest for the use of the money and must repay the entire amount of the bond at a specified time.

bull market A market in which stock prices are consistently rising.

capital appreciation The increase in the value of an investment over its original cost. Growth stocks offer the possibility of tremendous capital appreciation.

capital gains The profit made when securities are sold for more than their original purchase price.

commercial paper Corporate IOUs that are normally issued by established companies and that are due after 30 to 90 days.

dividend A portion of a company's earnings that is distributed to stockholders; the amount is determined by the board of directors.

earnings A company's revenues minus its costs, expenses, and taxes; figured before paying dividends.

earnings per share (EPS) A company's net profit divided by the number of shares of stock outstanding.

growth company A company characterized by expanding operations, increasing profits, excellent management, and a strong research and development program. The shares of growth companies are growth stocks.

growth industry An industry that is expanding through increased product sales or technological advancements.

growth stock A stock issued by a company that has sales and profits growing at a rate faster than the growth rate of its particular industry or of the economy in general.

income reinvestment rate A measure of a company's growth through internal financing; calculated by multiplying the company's return on equity by its income retention rate.

income retention rate The percentage of a company's earnings reinvested into the business rather than paid out in dividends.

income stock Shares of a company that provide regular dividend income rather than long-term growth in value.

inflation A rise in prices that causes money to lose purchasing power and interest rates to increase.

internal financing A company's use of its profits to fund its further expansion.

investment banker A person who arranges company financing through the issue of new stocks and bonds.

liabilities Debts, payments due to suppliers, salaries due to employees, and anything else that a company owes.

long-term investment Any investment in which capital gains will not be realized until several years have passed. Growth stocks are generally a long-term investment.

price/earnings ratio, P/E ratio The price of a share of stock divided by the earnings per share. The calculation is used to compare the cost of a stock to its earnings performance.

prime rate The interest rate charged by commercial banks to their most creditworthy customers, such as corporations.

profit or ***net income*** The amount of earnings remaining after a company pays all of its expenses.

return on equity (ROE) A measure of profitability that expresses the relationship between a company's net income and its stockholders' equity.

share of stock Any of the equal parts into which the entire value, or equity, of a company is divided.

short-term investment Any investment made to realize quick capital gains. Treasury bills are a short-term investment.

stockholders' equity The money that remains after a company's liabilities have been subtracted from its assets. Represents the stockholders' interest in the company.

stock split An increase in the number of outstanding shares in a company that does not change the total value of the shares.

Treasury bills (T-bills) Short-term (3-, 6-, or 12-month) U.S. government bonds.

venture capitalist An individual who provides money, known as "seed money," to start or expand a business and is willing to make a risky investment in the hope of making a large profit.

yield The return on an investment in the form of dividends or interest payments; expressed as a percentage of the current price.

FURTHER READING

Cappiello, Frank A. *Finding the Next Super Stock*. Cockeysville, MD: Liberty Publishing, 1982. Analyzes growth companies of the past and their stocks and outlines a method for identifying and predicting future growth stocks.

Ellis, Jack C. *A History of Film*. Englewood Cliffs, NJ: Prentice-Hall, 1979. A description of the evolution of the international movie industry as a business and as an art form.

Inc. Published by Inc. Publishing Corporation. This magazine about young companies also profiles the entrepreneurs who start and run them and analyzes market strategies, financial operations, and management styles as well.

Sachar, Laura. "The Fastest of the Largest." *Financial World*, August 25, 1987, p. 30. Provides analysts' choices of attractive large growth companies.

———. "Small Cap Stocks Worth the Risk." *Financial World*, August 25, 1987, p. 40. Highlights rapidly growing small companies.

Wensberg, Peter C. *Land's Polaroid: A Company and the Man Who Invented It*. Boston: Houghton Mifflin, 1987. An account of the company history and growth of Polaroid Corporation and of its founder, Edwin Herbert Land.

INDEX

JEFFREY B. LITTLE, a finance graduate of New York University, began his Wall Street career in the early 1960s. He has worked as an accountant for a retail brokerage firm, as an instructor of technical analysis in a broker training center, as a securities analyst of technology stocks, and as a portfolio manager and advisory committee member for a major mutual fund. He is a Fellow of the Financial Analysts Federation, a member of the New York Society of Security Analysts, and was formerly a vice-president of an investment counsel firm in Baltimore.

PAUL A. SAMUELSON, senior editorial consultant, is Institute Professor Emeritus at the Massachusetts Institute of Technology. He is author (now coauthor) of the best-selling textbook *Economics*. He served as an adviser to President John F. Kennedy and in 1970 was the first American to win the Nobel Prize in economics.

SHAWN PATRICK BURKE, consulting editor, is a securities analyst with Standard & Poor's Corporation. He has been an internal consultant in industry as well as for a Wall Street investment firm, and he has extensive experience in computer-generated financial modeling and analysis.

NANCY WELLES, contributing editor, is a free-lance writer and editor who specializes in business and finance. She did her undergraduate work at Antioch College and Sophia University (Tokyo) and received a master's degree from Teachers College, Columbia University.

ACKNOWLEDGMENTS Courtesy Abbott Laboratories: p. 43; The Bettmann Archive: pp. 11, 32; courtesy of Celestial Seasonings: p. 13; courtesy of Consolidated Edison of New York: p. 10; courtesy of Cray Research, Inc.: p. 22; Culver Pictures, Inc.: p. 33 (top); Drake Well Museum: p. 8; courtesy of *Financial World* magazine: pp. 20, 21; courtesy of Genentech, Inc.: p. 42; George Haling: cover; courtesy of International Business Machines Corporation: p. 18; © Lucasfilm Ltd.: p. 33 (bottom); Courtesy of Motorola: p. 26; courtesy of Polaroid Corporation: p. 24; courtesy of Sears: p. 22; Sharp: p. 29; UPI/Bettmann Newsphotos: pp. 23, 34, 35, 39.

The editors gratefully acknowledge the assistance given by Heather Goodchild of Standard & Poor's Corporation, New York, New York.